I0605997

To those who came for their own version of the American Dream

Many thanks to Anthony Salazar, chair of the Latino Baseball Committee, Society for American Baseball Research (SABR), for reviewing the text and illustrations.

Millbrook Press™
An imprint of Lerner Publishing Group, Inc.
241 First Avenue North
Minneapolis, MN 55401 USA

For reading levels and more information, look up this title at www.lernerbooks.com.

Designed by Danielle Carnito and Ramon Olivera.
Main body text set in Aptifer Slab LT Pro.
Typeface provided by Linotype AG.
The illustrations in this book were created with Adobe Illustrator and Adobe Photoshop.

Library of Congress Cataloging-in-Publication Data

Names: Olivera, Ramon, 1971– author illustrator
Title: Béisbol begins : how Nemesio Guilló brought baseball to Cuba / Ramon Olivera.
Description: Minneapolis : Millbrook Press, 2026. | Includes bibliographical references. | Audience: Ages 6–10 | Audience: Grades 2–3 | Summary: "When Nemesio Guilló traveled from his home in Havana, Cuba, to a school in Alabama, he didn't know he was going to fall in love with a new sport—baseball! Discover how this teenager brought baseball to Cuba"— Provided by publisher.
Identifiers: LCCN 2025019730 (print) | LCCN 2025019731 (ebook) | ISBN 9798765649343 library binding | ISBN 9798765699782 epub
Subjects: LCSH: Guilló, Nemesio—Juvenile literature | Baseball—Cuba—History—Juvenile literature | Baseball players—Cuba—Biography—Juvenile literature | LCGFT: Biographies
Classification: LCC GV865.G835 O58 2026 (print) | LCC GV865.G835 (ebook) | DDC 796.357092 [B]—dc23/eng/20250716

LC record available at https://lccn.loc.gov/2025019730
LC ebook record available at https://lccn.loc.gov/2025019731

Manufactured in Guang Dong, China by Dream Colour Printing
1-1012842-53544-6/25/2025

Béisbol Begins

How Nemesio Guilló Brought Baseball to Cuba

Ramon Olivera

Millbrook Press • Minneapolis

IN 1858,
on the island of Cuba,
in the city of Havana,
there lived a young boy named Nemesio.

Nemesio lived with his mother, his father, and his older brother, Ernesto. Their family owned a successful sugar factory. In those days, some wealthy families sent their children away to school. Nemesio's parents decided to send him and Ernesto to study in the United States.

The boys packed their trunks, said goodbye to their parents, and set sail across the Gulf of Mexico.

TENNESSEE
SOUTH CAROLINA
ARKANSAS
MISSISSIPPI
ALABAMA
GEORGIA
ATLANTIC OCEAN
TEXAS
LOUISIANA
MOBILE
FLORIDA
BAHAMA ISLANDS
GULF OF MEXICO
HAVANA
CUBA
JAMAICA
MEXICO
BELIZE
CARIBBEAN SEA
GUATEMALA
HONDURAS
EL SALVADOR
NICARAGUA
N
W
E
S

Nemesio had to adjust to many things in the United States.

The language was different.
The food was different.
And sometimes even the games were different.

A game called *baseball* was just beginning to become popular in the US when Nemesio and Ernesto arrived.

Nemesio had never seen anything like it before!
The boys watched closely as players gathered for a game.

A pitcher hurled a dark, leathery ball toward home base.

The batsman swung, sending the ball through the infield.

The outfielder scrambled to scoop it up and throw it toward the catcher.

The runner raced like a horse . . .
Around the bases . . .
Crossing home base . . .

To a "Hip, hip, hurrah!"

Nemesio dreamed of someday forming a team back home in Cuba. But, he wondered, would Spain ever allow such a game to be played there?

Cuba, which was known as the Pearl of the Antilles, was still a colony of Spain. The Spanish rulers expected the Cuban people to follow Spanish customs, like bullfighting.

Bullfighting was a violent sport in which the matador was a one-man team. He taunted, dodged, and speared the animal as it charged past. The fight was over when the matador, with cape and sword in hand, killed the bull with one final stab.

Cubans believed that bullfighting was a cruel, unfair, and old-fashioned custom.

Baseball, however, was new and exciting!

Baseball players worked together.
The teams were even.
The rules were fair.

Nemesio thought this new game was a better reflection of the spirit of the Cuban people.

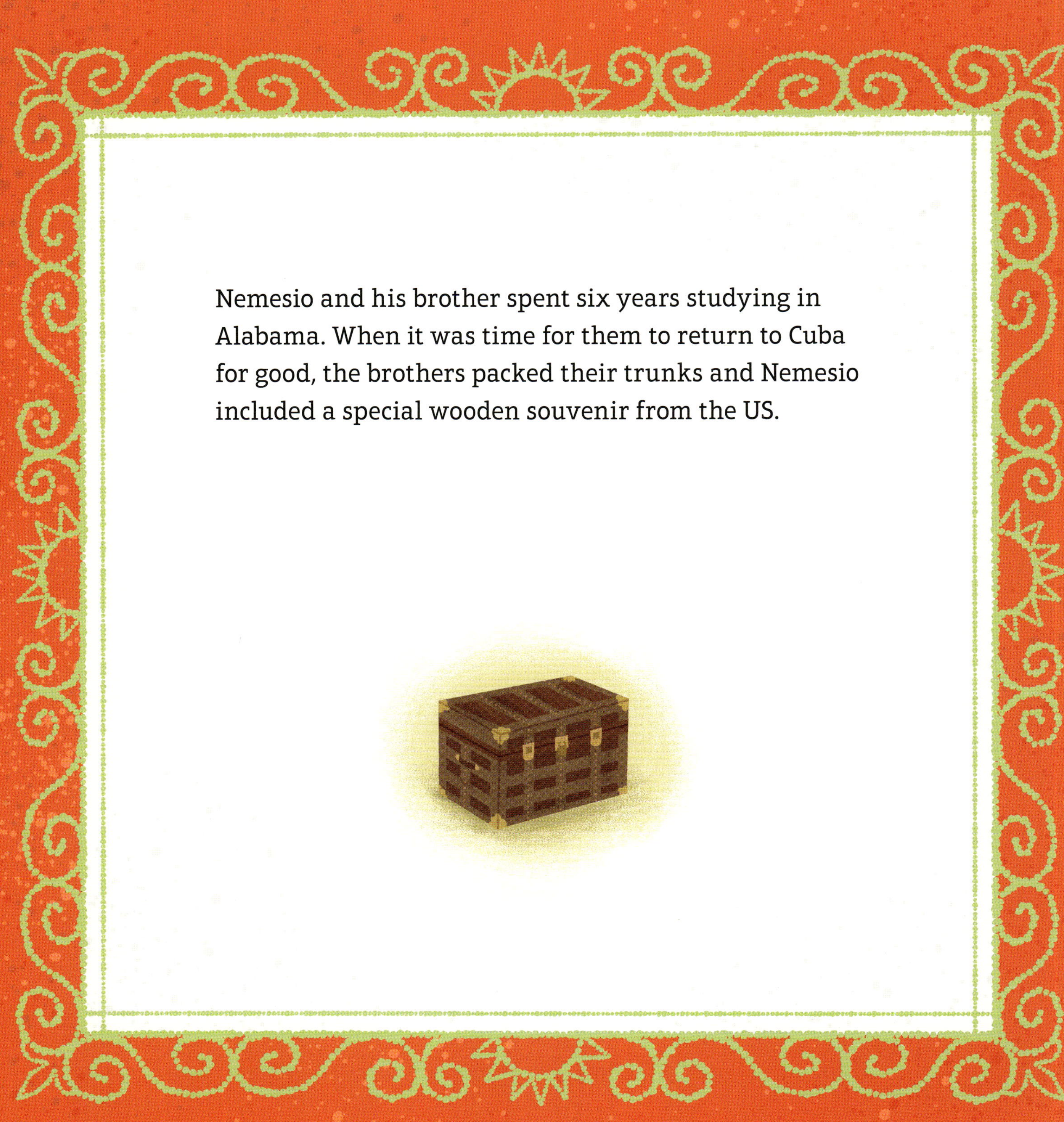

Nemesio and his brother spent six years studying in Alabama. When it was time for them to return to Cuba for good, the brothers packed their trunks and Nemesio included a special wooden souvenir from the US.

A steamship took Nemesio and Ernesto from Alabama, across the gulf, and all the way home to Havana. The boys couldn't wait to share all they had seen and done!

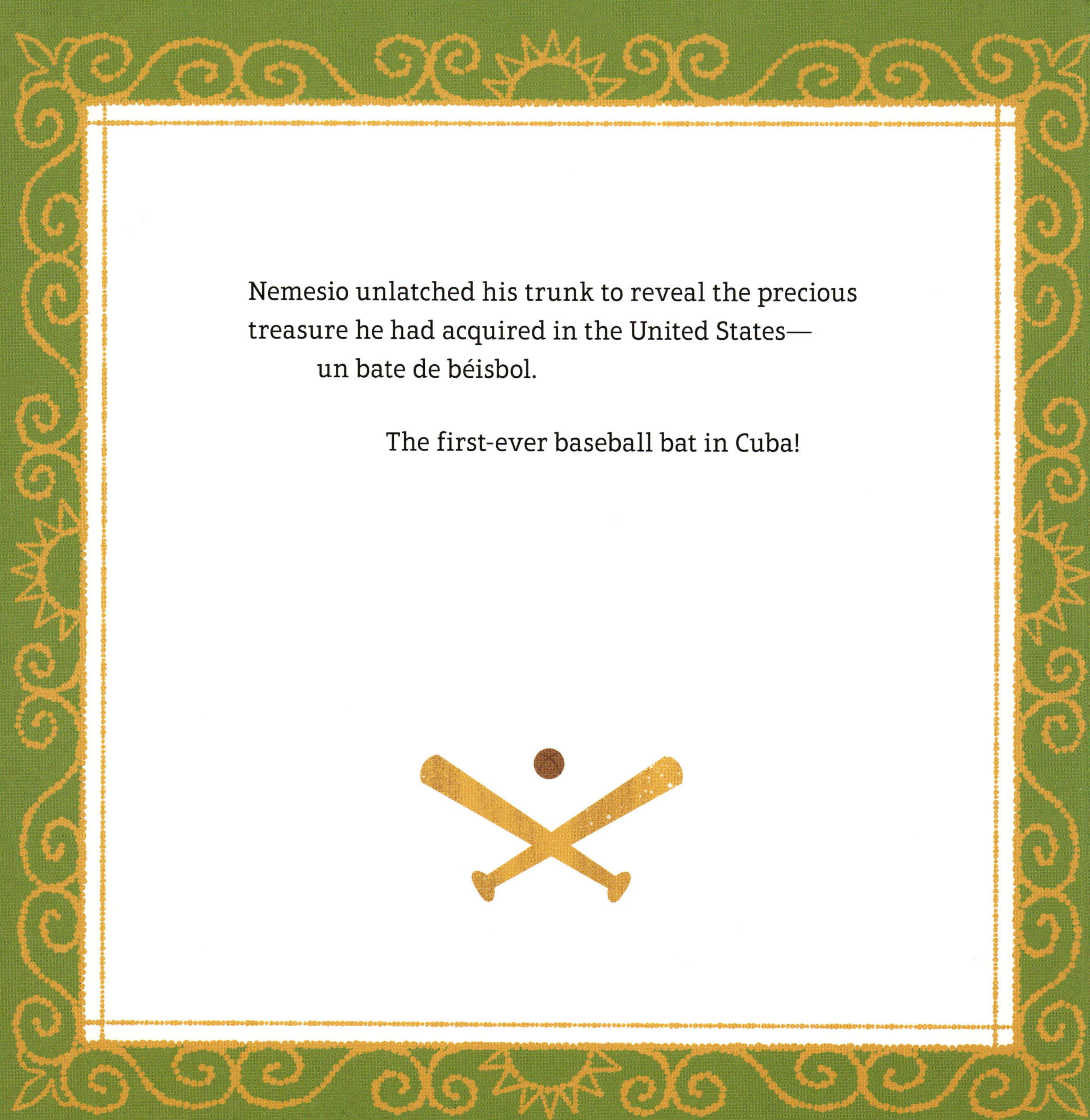

Nemesio unlatched his trunk to reveal the precious treasure he had acquired in the United States—
un bate de béisbol.

The first-ever baseball bat in Cuba!

With bat in hand, Nemesio gathered his friends to teach them all about this new game. They didn't have enough players for full teams, so they had to come up with their own way to play, but that didn't matter.

They were swinging and hitting.
They were running and throwing.
They were catching and tagging.

If a ball dropped into the outfield? Base hit!

If it was hit farther? ¡Un doble! A double!

If a ball was caught as it was falling out of a tree? You're out!

More and more peloteros joined Nemesio to play ball.

By 1868, he had helped form the first béisbol team in Cuba—
the Habana Base Ball Club.

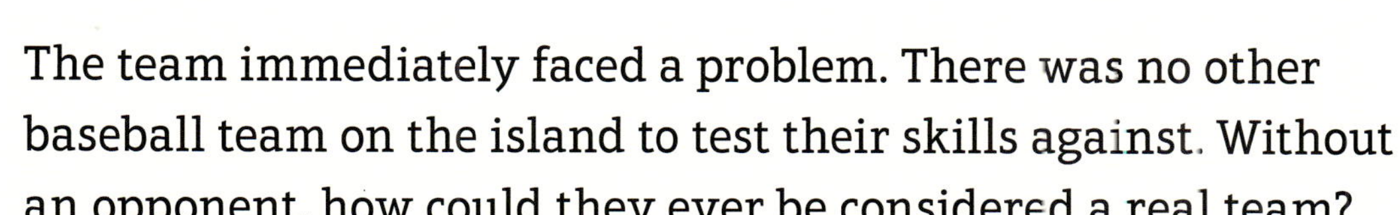

The team immediately faced a problem. There was no other baseball team on the island to test their skills against. Without an opponent, how could they ever be considered a real team?

When word came that a crew of American sailors were docked in the nearby port city of Matanzas, Nemesio and the Habana Base Ball Club traveled there to challenge them to a game.

For nine full innings,

they were swinging and hitting.
They were running and throwing.
They were catching and tagging . . .

. . . until the Habana Base Ball Club came out on top!

Nemesio and his teammates were finally a real baseball team.

In the years to come, baseball spread across Cuba like a hurricane. But the Spanish authorities looked at baseball with great suspicion.

Bats were seen as weapons.
Ball players were potential rebels.
Baseball became a threat to Spanish rule.

The Spanish governor banned the American sport from being played in Cuba.

For years, tensions grew between the Cuban people and their Spanish rulers. The government took advantage of Cubans and tried to control their lives. Cubans felt it was unfair that they had so little say in how their country was run.

Cubans could no longer stand to live under crushing Spanish rule. In 1895, they started a revolution. The Cuban War of Independence had begun. But Spain would not let go of its crown jewel that easily.

The United States joined the war on the side of the Cubans. With help from the US, Spain was quickly defeated and driven from Cuba.

Cuba gained its independence in 1902.

And, thanks to Nemesio and his bat,
béisbol became the national sport of Cuba.

ADOLFO LUQUE
PITCHER
MINNIE MIÑOSO
REDS
24
TONY PEREZ
A
A
RAFAEL ALMEIDA
HABANA
H
MARTÍN DIHIGO
Monarchs
JOSÉ MÉNDEZ
KANSAS CITY MONARCHS
ESTEBAN BELLÁN
Troy
CRISTÓBAL TORRIENTE
CHICAGO
ARMANDO MARSANS

MORE ABOUT THE HISTORY OF CUBA

The history of Spain's involvement with Cuba goes back many hundreds of years. Beginning with Christopher Columbus's first voyage to the Caribbean in 1492, Spain was heavily involved in colonizing the Caribbean as well as North and South America. It established Cuba as a colony in 1511. Within one hundred years, nearly the entire Indigenous population of Cuba had been killed through violence, forced labor, and disease. The Spanish then brought in enslaved Africans and forced them to work on plantations. Over the next few centuries, Cuba went on to become one of the most profitable colonies in the world. The island's fertile soil was well-suited for growing crops such as sugar and tobacco, which generated a lot of wealth for Spain. In addition, Havana's natural harbor gave Spain an advantage in shipping. By the end of the 1800s, Spain had lost nearly all of its other colonies in the Americas to independence movements. Yet it held on tightly to Cuba.

Although the colony was prosperous, its citizens were not treated fairly. Cubans were burdened with high taxes. They lacked representation in the government. Corruption and broken promises by the Spanish pushed Cubans to rebellion.

The Cuban War of Independence erupted in 1895. Cuban rebels were effective in wearing down the Spanish with guerrilla-style warfare. The Spanish countered with firing squads and concentration camps (relocating a third of the population). The explosion of the American battleship USS *Maine* in Havana Harbor, blamed on Spain, finally led the US to join the war in 1898. The Spanish–American War, as it was then known, ended a few months later with Spain defeated. The United States occupied Cuba for three years, granting its independence in 1902.

Cubans fleeing the war took baseball to other parts of Latin America, including Puerto Rico, Venezuela, and the Dominican Republic. As early as the 1870s, some Cubans were already playing professional baseball in the United States.

In the first half of the twentieth century, many Cubans went on to become stars in the Major Leagues and the Negro Leagues. Players from the United States took part in the Cuban winter league as well, creating further connections between the two countries through a shared love of the sport.

In 1959 Fidel Castro became the leader of Cuba, and in the following years he established himself as a dictator. Castro would not allow people to express themselves openly or leave the country freely. He also banned professional sports in Cuba—including baseball. Castro allowed only amateur baseball, in which players couldn't be paid. This made lots of players unhappy. In the decades since then, many talented Cuban ballplayers have come to the United States to pursue careers in las Grandes Ligas de Béisbol.

MORE ABOUT NEMESIO GUILLÓ

Historians don't know a lot of the details of Nemesio's early life, but records indicate that he was eleven years old in 1858, when he came to Mobile, Alabama, to attend Spring Hill College. Baseball was experiencing a surge in popularity in the United States in the middle of the 1800s, spread in part by soldiers fighting in the US Civil War (1861–1865). Both Nemesio and his brother, Ernesto, helped popularize the game in Cuba after their return home.

Cuba's first professional baseball league was created in 1878. Although Ernesto had retired from the sport by that point, Nemesio continued to play until about 1893. Records show that as a fielder, he played at second base, shortstop, and in right field. After his baseball career, he worked as a bookkeeper. He died in 1931 and was inducted into the Cuban Baseball Hall of Fame in 1948.

GLOSSARY

Antilles: (ahn-TEE-yays) a group of islands in the Caribbean Sea that includes Cuba, Hispaniola, Jamaica, and Puerto Rico

bate: (BAH-tay) bat

béisbol: (BASE-bohl) baseball

doble: (DOH-blay) double

Habana: (ah-BAH-nah) Havana, capital of Cuba

las Grandes Ligas de Béisbol: (lahs GRAHN-deis LEE-gahs day BASE-bohl) Major Leagues

matador: (mah-tah-DOHR) bullfighter

peloteros: (pay-loh-TAIR-ohs) baseball players

Salón de la Fama: (sah-LOHN day lah FAH-mah) Hall of Fame

FLAGS

Cuba

Spain

United States of America

BIBLIOGRAPHY

Bjarkman, Peter C. *Cuba's Baseball Defectors: The Inside Story*. Rowman & Littlefield, 2016.

Bjarkman, Peter C. *A History of Cuban Baseball, 1864–2006*. McFarland & Company, Inc., 2007.

Burgos, Adrian. *Cuban Star: How One Negro-League Owner Changed the Face of Baseball*. Hill and Wang, 2011.

González Echevarría, Roberto. *The Pride of Havana: A History of Cuban Baseball*. Oxford University Press, 1999.

Pi, Guillermo. "Nemesio Guilló Fué Quien Trajo a Cuba el Primer Bate y la Primera Pelota" in: *Diario de la Marina*. Havana, Cuba, January 6, 1924.